BLOCK PRINTING

BLOCK PRINTING

Basic Techniques for Linoleum and Wood

Sandy Allison, editor
instruction and art by Robert Craig
photographs by Alan Wycheck

STACKPOLE
BOOKS

Published by
STACKPOLE BOOKS
5067 Ritter Road
Mechanicsburg, PA 17055
www.stackpolebooks.com

Printed in the United States of America

10 9 8 7 6 5 4 3 2 1

First edition

Cover design by Tessa J. Sweigert
Cover block print, "Juniper," by Robert Craig

Library of Congress Cataloging-in-Publication Data

Block printing : basic techniques for linoleum and wood / Sandy
Allison, editor ; featuring instruction and art by Robert Craig ;
photographs by Alan Wycheck. — 1st ed.
    p. cm.
  ISBN 978-0-8117-0601-8
  1. Linoleum block-printing—Technique. 2.
Wood-engraving—Printing—Technique. I. Allison, Sandy. II. Craig,
Robert, 1959–
  NE1330.B56 2011
  761—dc22
                                    2011000225

Contents

Beginnings

Block printing is a centuries-old art form first practiced in Japan, China, India, Korea, and elsewhere. It can be used to create fine art prints, illustrations, greeting cards, gift wrapping, posters, advertisements, and numerous other graphic works on paper. It can be done on fabric as well. While many block prints have a distinctive look and spirit, they can vary widely, from simple and bold to delicate and filigreed.

Traditionally, blocks for printing have been carved from wood, but they can also be created from linoleum, which is relatively inexpensive and readily available. (Both materials are suitable for making fine art prints: Pablo Picasso and Henri Matisse worked extensively with linoleum, as did the German Expressionists and artists at the Grosvenor School of Modern Art in London.) Tools and carving techniques for wood and linoleum are similar but differ in important ways; hand-printing techniques are basically the same.

This book covers the basics of working with both linoleum and wood. It starts with selecting sketches that would work well as block prints and demonstrates an easy way to transfer sketches to the surface of a block. It covers carving tools and the proper ways to carve linoleum then moves on to inking techniques. Printing by hand and pulling a print are covered in detail, as are editioning and registration and clean-up techniques.

Selecting wood and the tools and techniques for carving it are also described, as is a way to make multicolored reduction prints. The book also describes the different types of paper suitable for printmaking. It ends with a gallery of finished prints that include notations by the artist, printmaker Robert Craig.

Getting started block printing is easy, and the materials and tools are readily available. As with any craft, it's best to start small at first then tackle larger and more complex projects. This book will cover everything you need to know to make original and practical works of art.

1 Transferring an Image

Linoleum for printing is available at most art stores and craft centers or online and usually comes mounted on a 3/4-inch-thick block of plywood, ready to carve. The linoleum itself—a mixture of cork and linseed oil—has no grain, so it's easy to cut in any direction. It can hold fairly fine detail. Linoleum blocks are often gray (so-called "battleship gray") or tan. The white material shown here is printing foam—very easy to cut with a pencil or skewer and inexpensive, it is good for practice or younger artists.

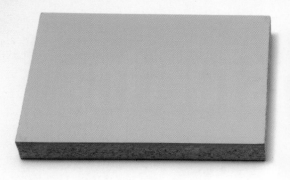
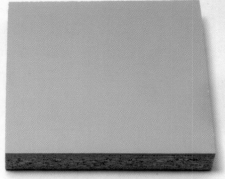

Linoleum blocks come in a variety of standard square or rectangular sizes: 4 by 5 inches, 5 by 7, 8 by 10, and 9 by 12 are most common. If you want to make a print that's not a standard size, it's a simple matter to cut down a standard linoleum block using a handsaw or table saw.

Battleship gray linoleum also comes unmounted in square or rectangular pieces or rolls. The advantage to buying this form is that it's slightly cheaper and more easily cut down. Unmounted linoleum is almost always mounted before carving, however, by gluing it to a plywood block using a heavy-duty adhesive.

Block printing linoleum also comes in a "gold-cut" variety. This material is slightly softer than battleship gray and a touch easier to cut. Like the gray, it has no grain. Alternative block-cutting products are also available; many of these are even softer than gold-cut but can't be worked to show fine detail.

"Linoleum" Flooring

The material on the surface of linoleum blocks is similar to the true linoleum still used as a flooring material. But much of what is today thought of as flooring linoleum is actually vinyl and nothing like printing linoleum. Early linocut artists used true linoleum flooring material to make prints, and it's possible for you to do the same. Be aware, however, that older linoleum made before the 1970s often contains asbestos and should not be carved.

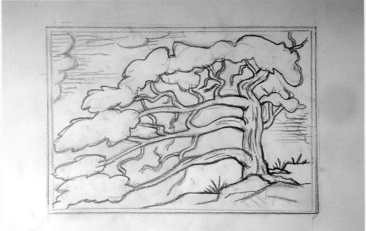

Almost any sketched image can be made into a block print, but all will require at least some abstraction to be rendered successfully. This pencil drawing of a juniper tree features a simplified branching pattern, clumps of foliage instead of individual leaves, and the suggestion of a darkening sky around the clouds. The sketch must be rendered "in black and white" (if not literally, at least metaphorically); you must decide for every stroke, line, dot, or segment whether it will print or not—there's no in-between. If it's going to print, it must not be cut away. If it's cut away, it will not print.

A comparison of sketches and finished prints helps show the range of subjects that can be rendered as prints, and how sketches are altered during carving. Note how this stand of trees in the snow was sketched so it could be reproduced as a block print. The shadows and background trees are solid black with highlights cut out to indicate texture. The places where the branches cross in front of other branches and the sky are solid black so they don't "disappear." When you work up a sketch for a print, think carefully how each element will be rendered in a print.

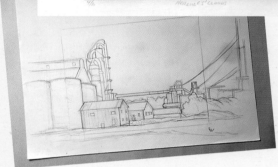

Even though it's printed in two colors, this industrial scene was abstracted before it could be suitably rendered in ink. The shadows on the buildings and the stormy clouds are represented by carved bands of varying widths. The trees are solid with carved streaks indicating branches and leaves. The large pipe was left solid where it crosses the sky and cut away where it crosses the background trees. Notice, too, how the image was cropped and the edges of the block drawn in on the sketch—the artist focused on what was most important and composed the image that was to be printed.

Tracing paper is used to transfer a pencil sketch to the surface of a linoleum block. (An alternate method described on page 10 uses carbon paper). The same methods for transferring sketches to linoleum blocks can also be used for wood blocks.

Pencils with relatively soft lead, available at art and craft stores, are used. The 6B pencil here is fairly soft; the 2B pencil approaches the medium range.

Transfer Process

1 The first step in transferring a sketch is to cover it with a piece of tracing paper cut to exact size.

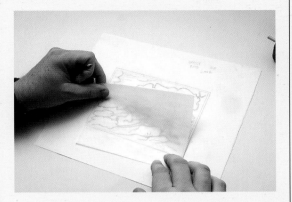

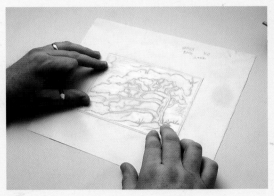

2 Tape the tracing paper down at the four corners using masking tape. Don't use transparent tape; it's too difficult to remove.

3 Trace the sketch onto the tracing paper using a soft 6B pencil.

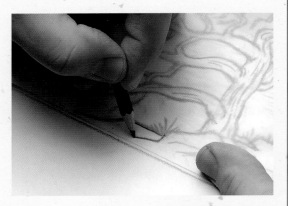

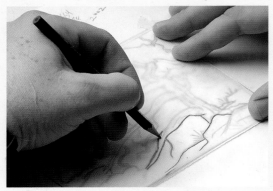

You can transfer the sketch in detail, or simply roughly indicate where different cuts will go.

4 Next, remove the tape and tracing paper from the sketch.

5 Flip the tracing paper over so the drawn-on side is facing the linoleum.

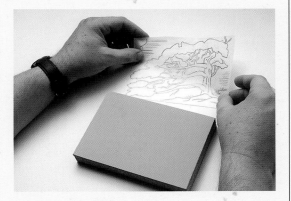

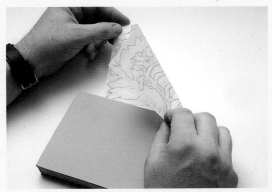

6 Align the edges of the tracing paper with the edges of the block.

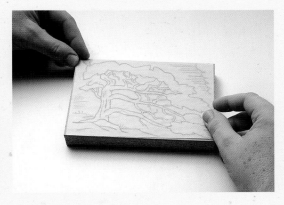

7 Tape it down using masking tape.

Remember that the carved block will show a mirror image of how the print will appear.

8 Carefully draw over all the lines using a 6B pencil.

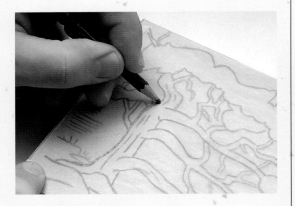

The idea is to transfer the lead marks on the underside of the paper to the linoleum. The soft 6B marks transfer much more easily than would marks made with a harder lead.

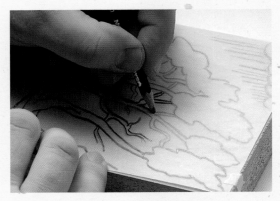

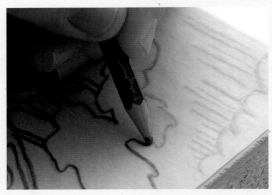

Press firmly, and draw directly on top of the lines so they transfer as completely as possible.

9 Check to see that all lines transferred by pulling up a corner or two of the tracing paper.

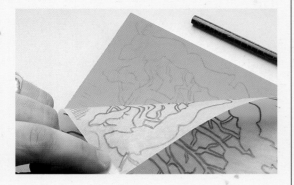

10 If something didn't transfer, retape the tracing paper and redraw the missed lines.

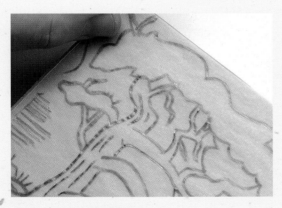

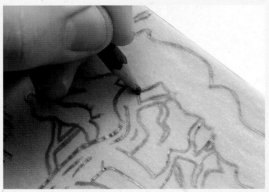

11 When you're finished, remove the tracing paper from the block.

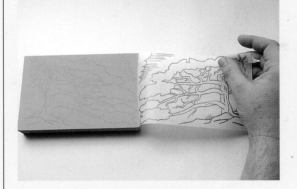

If you've drawn carefully, the sketch should be completely and accurately transferred to the linoleum surface.

An Alternate Transfer Method

You can also transfer a sketch to a linoleum block by photocopying the drawing using the copier's mirror image setting (you can also enlarge or reduce the sketch if needed) then placing it over a piece of carbon paper and taping both to the block. You can then draw over all the lines with a 2B pencil. It works best if both the photocopy and carbon paper are cut down to the same size as the block. Don't forget to place the carbon paper with the ink side toward the block.

Some artists begin carving at this point, but many use a marker to go over the drawing once again so all the outlines are bold and easy to see and won't smear or fade. Get markers of varying widths: Use a finer point to outline small drawings, a medium for larger drawings, and a broad marker to darken areas that will print (as explained in chapter 2).

12 Redraw all the lines on the block with the marker.

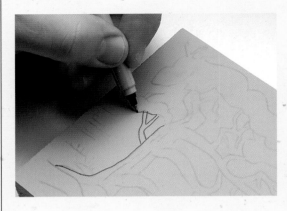

It's up to you how closely you follow the sketch. When you cut, the lines and shapes will most likely shift somewhat anyway. That's the nature—and the charm—of a block print.

Some artists painstakingly redraw the sketch. Others use the bold lines simply as guidelines to help them when they carve.

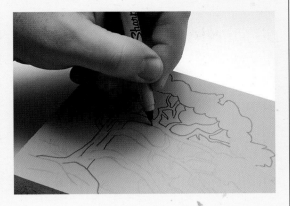

13 Traditional block prints usually feature a solid border all around the image. Use the marker to draw a line about ¼ to ½ inch away from the edge of the block.

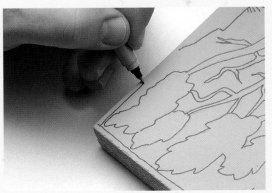

This border helps frame the image. It will be left uncarved.

After the drawing is bold enough to see clearly, the next step is to carve the block.

A side-by-side comparison of the block with the transferred sketch and the block after it's been carved and inked shows how much variation and detail can be added during the carving process.

Notice in particular how the "blank" sky was given movement and energy by leaving parts of it uncarved. Notice, too, how the "solid" trunk was carved with a few lines to create depth.

As you gain experience, you'll be able to visualize how the sketched-in image can be carved to create the look you're after.

2 Carving a Linoleum Block

A variety of tools for carving linoleum (and wood blocks) are available. They range from inexpensive linoleum cutting tools meant to be replaced after they become worn to costly tempered steel tools that can be sharpened and used almost forever. Linoleum dulls a sharp tool faster than wood does; lino-cutting and wood-cutting tools are not interchangeable.

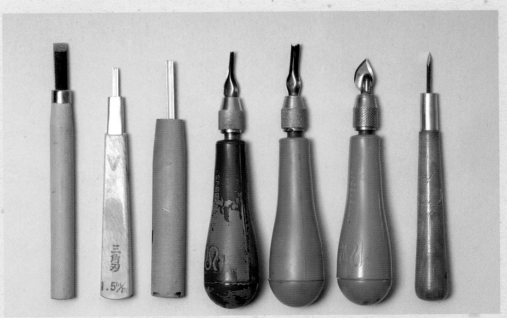

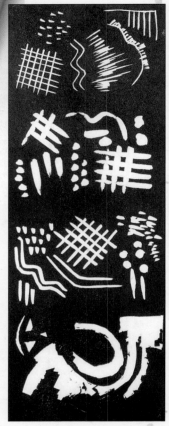

The most useful tools are U-shaped and V-shaped gouges: they can be used to make most of the cuts you'll need for linoleum carving. Knives—used more for wood carving—have limited use for linocuts, but some artists like to have them handy.

Speedball makes a line of tools specifically for lino cutting: They are available in a variety of textures and widths. These tools are usually called veiners and range from size 1 to 5, with 5 being the largest. Tool 6 is a knife.

Different shapes and sizes of gouges make different cuts. The cuts at the top of the sample were made with a #1 veiner; those just below were made with a #5 veiner. The cuts at the bottom were made with a #6 knife; those just above were made with a #3 veiner.

If you're just starting out in linoleum carving, inexpensive, replaceable blades and a handle or two will work just fine. In fact, many experienced carvers get along fine with just these tools.

You'll find that a small brush and dustpan are useful to clear away the carved bits.

Good Carving Technique

Proper grip and hand position is important. Hold the carving tool in the palm of your hand with the first finger on top of the tool screw or neck of the blade.

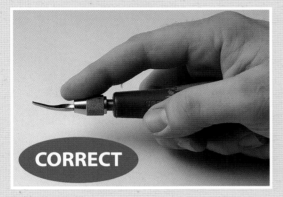

CORRECT

Don't hold the tool in your fist.

WRONG

Never position your free hand in front of the carving tool, as shown here. If you do and the cutting blade slips, you'll gouge your hand. Proper hand position is especially important when you're carving wood, as the tools tend to be much sharper. Slips are, unfortunately, common on both linoleum and wood, so it's best to be prepared.

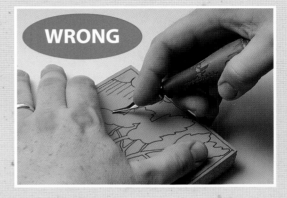

WRONG

This technique is doubly wrong: the free hand is in front of the tool, and the tool is held at too great an angle to the linoleum surface.

WRONG

Cutting Carefully

1 It is usually helpful, though not always necessary, to use the free hand to help guide the blade as it cuts.

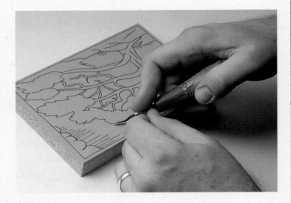

2 To help guide the cutting stroke, place the tip of the first finger of the free hand on the top of the gouge. Push the blade forward to cut, pressing down slightly. The free hand also serves to hold the block in place.

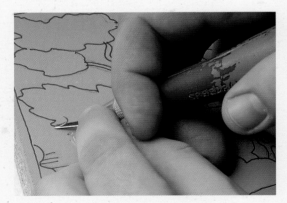

The small U-shaped gouge here removes tiny slices of linoleum.

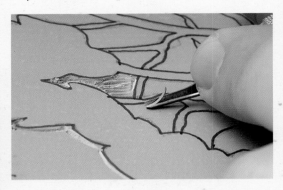

3 Start out removing only small pieces of material—you can always cut more.

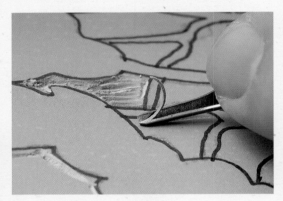

4 Don't cut deeply into the linoleum. You need to remove only a shallow slice: that's enough to make a cut that won't print.

Never wiggle the tool to help make it cut. Doing so can create a miscut or slip.

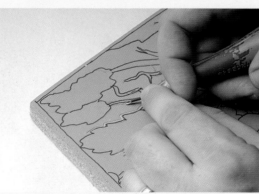

5 You can start carving anywhere, removing the linoleum you want to remove and keeping what you want to print untouched.

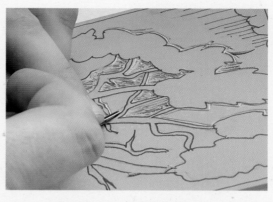

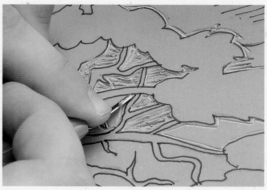

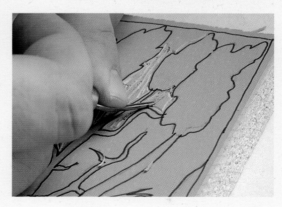

Remember that a hallmark of many block prints is that the areas that aren't meant to print still have interesting texture. Lines and streaks are left uncut to show on the printed image. These add energy and indicate the handcrafted, graphic quality of the piece. Of course, you can always remove all the linoleum surface from areas that aren't supposed to print if you prefer a clean look.

Larger gouges will remove more material in one stroke.

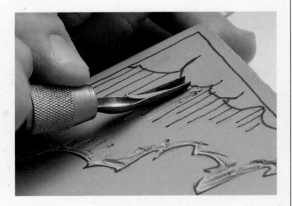

6 As you cut, you'll need to turn the block quite often in order to keep pushing the blade away from you.

7 Notice how the streaking in the sky is accomplished. The wider U-shaped gouge is used to make roughly parallel bands.

8 Then the gouge is used cut away an outline of the cloud.

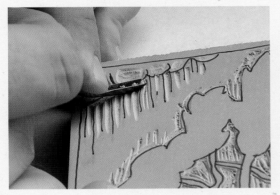

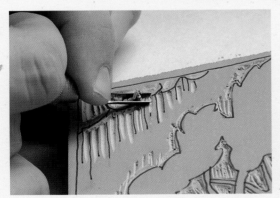

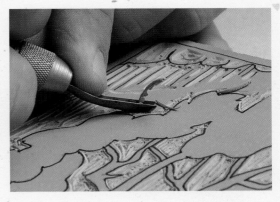

9 As you gain experience, you'll recognize how combinations of cuts will look once they're printed.

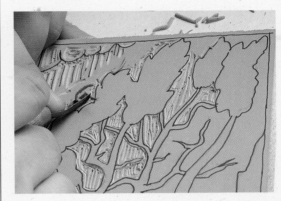

10 You'll achieve the best results if you make your cuts slowly and deliberately, never cutting too much or extending your cutting hand too far out in front of you.

11 Use the brush to remove all the trimmings from the linoleum and your work surface (it's helpful to have a wastebasket handy).

12 Use a broad-tip marker to darken all the uncut surface in order to help you visualize what the printed piece will look like. If you wish, you can darken areas as you cut to help guide you.

Half the block here was cut and darkened, and half was left uncut.

13 Make any additional cuts you want until the carving is just the way you want it.

Tiny cuts in large, dark areas indicate highlights and create texture.

When the carving is complete, you're ready to prepare your paper and then print.

Choosing Paper

Selecting paper for a linocut or wood block print can be a daunting task—or a lot of fun—depending on your perspective. There is a wide variety of paper from which to choose, both machine made and handcrafted. In general, paper that's good for block printing is strong and absorbent, but not so absorbent that ink bleeds into it. Many artists use handmade Japanese "washi" paper, especially when employing traditional printing techniques. This paper usually contains fibers from gampi, kozo, or mitsumata plants.

Following is a short list of papers with varying characteristics and appearances—any would be a good choice for block printing.

Masa. A good all-around paper suitable for both water- and oil-based inks. Also serves as excellent proofing paper.

Mulberry. A warm natural paper, available in large sizes for bigger prints, or it can easily be torn down. Takes ink well and is strong enough to handle multiple printings.

Hosho. A beautiful, rich, white paper. Excellent for both water-based and oil-based ink.

Okowara. A natural paper that is strong and durable—known especially for its warm appearance. Also comes in large sheets. A student-grade version of Okowara is less expensive but slightly more difficult to work with.

Kitakata. A very strong and warm natural paper. A good all-around performer.

Unryu White. A pearly paper with visible fibers running through it, giving it a distinctive appearance. Excellent for block printing.

Rives BFK. A European paper that is heavier than Japanese papers—very durable, but more demanding for hand printing. Takes ink very well and is available in large sheets.

Rives Lightweight. Available in white or buff, this is not as heavy as the BFK and is somewhat less expensive. A good performer.

Nideggen. An excellent warm paper, especially good for black-and-white prints.

Most printing-paper retailers offer sample books so you can see what's available. Some websites feature detailed descriptions of paper uses and characteristics. Check them out, and visit shops that specialize in paper. Take a look at everything that's for sale and ask a lot of questions.

Tearing Paper

Traditionally, paper for printing is always torn down to size by hand, never cut with scissors or a knife. Use a long metal ruler to help you make the tear.

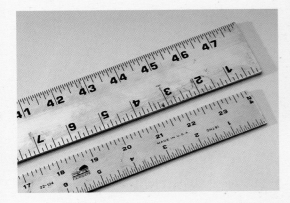

1 To tear a large sheet of paper into quarters, first measure halfway across the long edge and lay a ruler at this point, extending to the halfway point of the opposite edge. Near the top edge of the paper, make a tiny pencil mark.

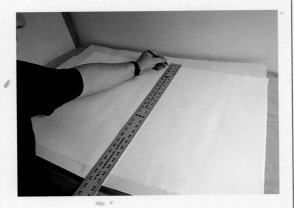

2 Do the same near the bottom edge.

3 Hold the ruler in place along the two marks.

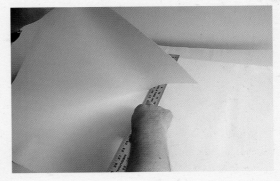

Japanese Paper

Most Japanese papers have a rough side and a smooth side. Printing is usually done on the rough side.

4 With the other hand, carefully tear the paper along the edge of the ruler that's on the marks.

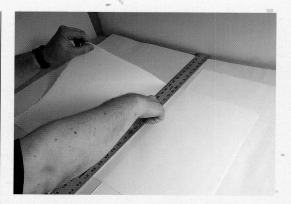

5 Make a slow, even tear, holding the ruler firmly in place on the work surface.

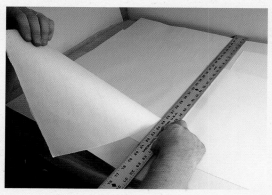

6 Measure halfway along the long sides of the torn pieces and rip them in half using the same technique.

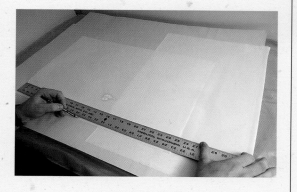

Measuring and tearing carefully will allow you to create sheets of uniform size, which is important for registering prints accurately.

3 Printing an Image by Hand

Printing block prints by hand instead of using a press can yield excellent results. A simple jig made of two strips of wood set in a 90-degree angle and screwed to a piece of plywood will work well for hand printing. Note the extra strips added alongside the shorter strip: these will allow you to set up a number of different ways to keep paper positioned so that you can print in the same area of every piece or create multicolored prints using multiple blocks or the reduction technique (described in the next chapter).

A very simple way to align smaller pieces of paper on the jig uses just masking tape and a pencil. The first step is to position a torn-down piece of paper on the jig so that the block will print in the center. (In general, it's best to leave generous margins around the printed portion of a finished piece—at least 3 or so inches for the smallest prints; more for larger ones.)

1 Hold the paper in place with one hand and stick a piece of tape to the jig as shown with the other; the tape should be underneath the corner of the paper.

2 Holding the paper in place, apply another piece of tape to the jig so that the top edge of the paper overlaps it.

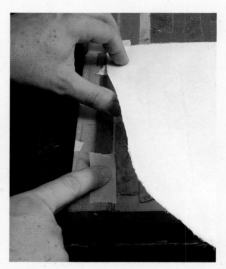

3 On this piece of tape, draw a line along the top edge of the paper, as shown.

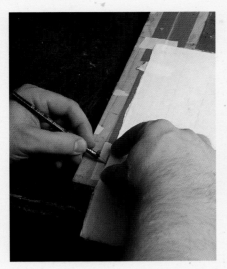

4 On the other piece, mark a right angle along the paper's corner.

You can now place a number of same-size sheets so the printed image will be centered the same way on each. This is an effective way to position single-color pieces, but it won't work well for work that includes multiple printings—there are more accurate registration methods for this.

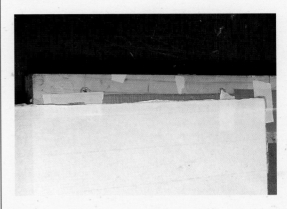

The Inking Process

Ink is best rolled out on a piece of glass. It's easy to make your own ink-rolling surface by taping a piece of standard window glass to a piece of plywood using heavy-duty duct tape. Here, a piece of white paper was laid underneath the glass before taping. This surface is around 18 by 12 inches. Don't use plexiglass.

1 The first step is to squeeze or scoop out a dollop of ink onto the rolling surface. In general, a 1- to 2-inch-long segment will be enough.

2 Slowly roll out the ink with the brayer. (See the next page for information on brayers.)

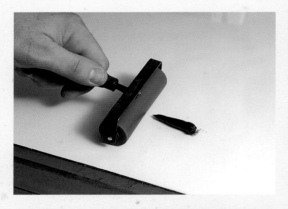

3 Allow some of the ink to cover the edges of the tool.

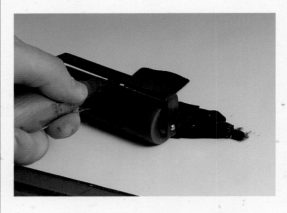

4 Roll smoothly using even pressure, but don't press so hard that the brayer slips. Roll the tool in different directions, creating a large, smooth ink surface on the glass.

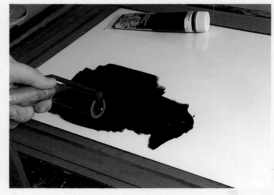

Water-based vs. Oil-based Inks

Ink for block printing is either water-based or oil-based. Both kinds are available in tubes or cans, and both come in a variety of premade colors. The main differences between water and oil are "open time," permanency, and cleanup.

Oil-based inks have a lengthy "open time"—they stay wet and workable for a long period of time after they're rolled—at least several hours and up to a day (the package will include exact information on open times). This means you can make prints over a long period of time. Oil-based ink is also permanent. You can apply watercolors on top of dried oil prints without smearing them. The biggest drawback to oil-based ink is that it can be messy and takes longer to clean off of the blocks, brayers, and rolling surface after a printing session.

Many water-based inks are not permanent or lightfast—watercolors used over top of even dry prints will smear them. Also, water-based inks dry quickly unless extenders are added and so you must work continuously during a printing session: you can't take a break without cleaning everything up before you stop and rolling out new ink when you resume printing. Cleanup of water-based inks is simple, however, and you can stack printed pieces after a brief drying time (as little as 30 minutes).

There are a few types of water-based inks on the market that are lightfast and have a longer open time than typical water-based inks. Look for these if the benefits of working with water-based ink appeal to you.

No matter which kind of ink you use, the process of inking the block and printing is exactly the same.

If you use ink from a can, use a spatula to scoop it out. The spatula could be plastic or metal.

Ink brayers for block printing are available in different sizes. A medium brayer about 4 inches wide is a versatile choice. The hardness of a brayer's surface is sometimes measured in durometers. Soft 20-durometer brayers are the preferred choice for most block printing. A harder 30-durometer brayer works well to ink blocks that have fine detailing; it has less of a tendency to fill in delicate areas.

The idea is to coat the brayer with an even, thin coat of ink. Too much ink will fill in block details.

5 When the ink starts to crackle as you roll it, you know you're ready to ink the block. This is known as "charging" the brayer.

Mixing Ink Colors

Both water- and oil-based inks can be mixed with other colors of the same kind (don't mix water- and oil-based inks together, however). Mixing allows you to create an almost infinite variety of colors. Mix ink in a separate container and then spread it on the rolling surface. Or mix directly on the surface using a flexible spatula or painter's mixing knife.

6 Roll the ink onto the surface of the block, rolling in all directions.

7 Work slow and deliberately to ensure that the entire uncut surface of the block is covered with a layer of ink.

Areas that are inked will look shiny when they are sufficiently coated.

The ink should evenly coat the roller with no globs that will fill in the cut-out areas of the block when it's printed.

8 When the block surface has an even coating of ink, set the block ink-side-up in the right angle of the jig, as shown.

9 Carefully hold the top edge of the paper on the raised part of the jig with the corner and top edge in line with the registration marks.

10 Lower the piece of paper onto the block.

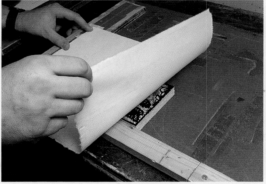

You'll find that the wet ink on the block will hold the paper in place somewhat.

11 To print, hold the paper lightly in place with one hand, and with the other, gently rub the backside of the paper with the rubbing tool, pressing it against the block (see next page for information on tools).

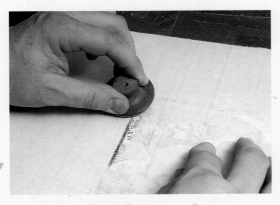

12 Work deliberately with controlled strokes so that every inked portion of the block transfers.

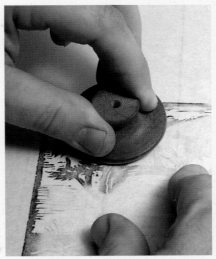

Transfer Tools

The key tool used to make a print is a baren—a smooth, slightly rounded object that presses the paper onto the inked surface of the block. An effective "baren" can be as simple is an old wooden doorknob or the underside of the bowl of a wooden spoon or as complex as an artfully constructed bamboo implement made especially for block printing (and, in some cases, very costly).

13 You don't have to press hard. Doing so can make a bruise or possibly a hole in the paper.

14 And you don't want to angle the tool so that its edge accidentally presses the paper into the cut-away portions of the block. Doing this can tear even the strongest paper.

15 The rubbing tool should glide evenly over the surface of the paper.

16 On many thinner printing papers, you will be able to see clearly what's being transferred.

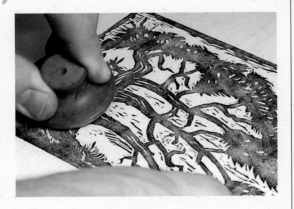

When you're finished transferring the ink, it's time to pull the print.

16 Set the rubbing tool down, hold the paper in place where it lies on the raised portion of the jig, and gently lift the far edge of the paper off the block.

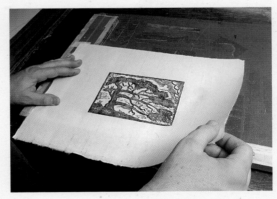

17 Pull the paper off the block in a slow, smooth, even motion.

The print is now complete. It just needs to dry.

Drying Prints

Just-printed work should be laid flat until it is dry. Drying racks, which can be somewhat costly, allow you to dry a lot of prints in a small space. Or you can simply lay the work out on a large table—it can't be stacked until the ink has dried completely.

Cleaning Up

Cleanup of water-based ink is easy, especially if you use a spray bottle filled with water.

1 Spritz the rolling surface and wipe it with paper towels.

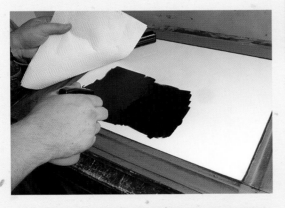

Cleanup of Oil Inks

Oil-based inks clean up in much the same way, but you'll need to use a solvent specially made for the purpose. Follow the instructions on the packaging when using such solvents. Choose a nontoxic and odorless solvent if you're working in an area with poor ventilation.

Mineral spirits, vegetable oil, and even nonstick cooking sprays can be used to clean oil-based inks too, with varying effectiveness.

2 Spritz again and wipe until the surface is clean.

3 To clean the brayer, roll it briskly on scrap paper or newspapers; this will remove much of the ink.

4 Roll the edges, too.

5 Then spritz the brayer with water and wipe with a paper towel. Washing the tools in a utility sink would work well, too.

Remember that when it's not in use, a brayer should be stored resting on its handle with the roller's surface facing up. This will prevent the surface from getting indented or otherwise marred.

Spritz and wipe the surface of the block and store it leaning upwards as shown so any dampness can dry easily.

Cleaned and dried blocks can be reused many times before the carving begins to wear down.

Editioning

Fine art prints are almost always editioned—printed in a limited quantity (known as an edition) and numbered within that edition. Of course, during a printing session, some prints might not turn out well and are discarded, so the total number in the edition doesn't necessarily reflect the number of pulls attempted. Block prints are typically made in editions of as many as fifty or as few as five.

The print's title is written in the center, along the bottom.

Traditionally, the individual print's number and the total number in the edition are written in pencil on the unprinted paper at the bottom left side of the print. Note that the individual print numbers don't necessarily reflect the order in which the prints were pulled.

The print is signed at the bottom right side.

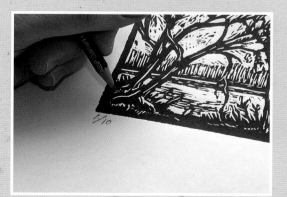

"Artist's proofs" are generally the first one or two successfully pulled prints; they are used to compare against the pulls that follow. Artist's proofs are not part of the edition total and are simply labeled AP.

Some artists also make BAT *(bon a tirer)* prints, which are also used to proof the prints in an edition.

Trimming the Paper

If the paper needs to be trimmed after a print is made, tear it down with the help of a metal ruler. Tearing paper properly is a process every block printer should know. Remember that margins around prints should be wide enough to accommodate framing and reframing. Large margins are the norm and often show off the beauty and artistry of a block print best.

Here, to make margins 3¾ inches wide, a margin is measured out from the edge of the print and marked.

1 Lay the ruler along the margin line.

2 Carefully tear off the excess paper along the ruler.

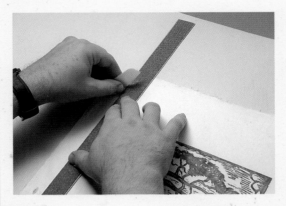

Mounting Prints

To mount a finished block print, using photo corners (available at craft centers, art stores, or online) will keep the print from being marred by tape or adhesive.

If you do use tape, choose acid-free or archival types. Attach the print to the backing with only a small bit of tape on the printing paper and you won't have to cut away much paper if you remount the image later.

Mounted prints can be matted with generous margins, or left unmatted and simply framed.

3 Repeat the process as needed until the margins are as you want them.

In this case, the side and top margins are all $3^3/_4$ inches; the bottom margin is slightly wider, around 4 inches, to accommodate the edition number, title, and artist's signature.

4 Making a Reduction Print

Reduction prints can be simple or complex, demanding extensive preplanning and careful execution. Making a reduction print involves cutting highlights out of a linoleum or wood block then printing a base color with it, cutting more away from the same block, and printing it again with a second color. The process is repeated as many times as is feasible. This technique allows the artist to make a multi-colored image using only one block. Of course, once the final color is printed, no more images can be made, since the carvings that made the preceding prints no longer exist.

The final print shown here was made with two colors on white paper: the first color was a golden brown and the second was black. Working from light to dark in the reduction process gives the best results.

After the rough image is transferred to the block, the first step is to carve away only those areas that won't print at all. In this case, that means carving out the white highlights.

1 Here, the highlights are limited to small areas along the neck and side of the face and nose and the eyes. Highlights were also added sparingly to the background to contrast with the edge of the face.

2 Remember that whatever you carve first in the reduction print process won't print at all—the paper will show through.

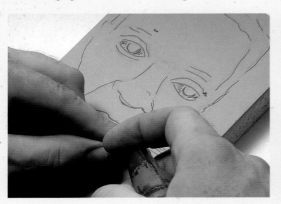

3 The highlights on this piece consist of short strokes made with a small U-gouge.

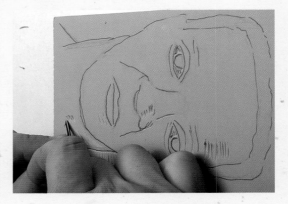

Don't go overboard and cut too much away, which would create too many highlights. The highlighting should be somewhat subtle.

4 The next step is to roll out the ink for the first color and charge the brayer.

5 Then coat the block with ink using the brayer.

Accurate registration is important for reduction prints. A pair of registration pins taped to the raised wood portion of the jig work well. The pins are affixed to the jig a few inches apart for smaller prints, as shown; they should be farther apart for larger prints.

These pins are available through printing or silk-screen material suppliers.

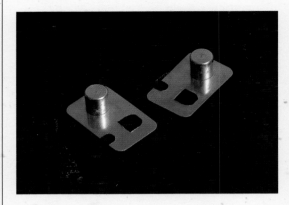

6 To use this registration method, the paper for the print will need to be slightly longer than the desired final margin on the side of the paper where the pins are. The paper can be torn down to final size after all the printing is complete.

Press the paper over the pins so they poke through; then reinforce the paper by pressing small pieces of masking tape over each pin and sticking it to the paper. This will prevent the holes from enlarging during the second (and subsequent) printing.

Two pins are sufficient for all but the largest prints.

7 Lift the paper up and set the inked block in place in the angle of the jig. Then use a baren to transfer the image.

8 Slowly pull the print.

Create enough first printings to complete the edition—it's wise to make a few extras to account for any that might be botched in the process. Remember that after you've carved the block for the printing of the second color, you can't go back and print the first color the same way you did before. If you want an edition of ten, you'll want to make at least twelve or thirteen first printings.

9 To prepare the block for the second printing, clean off the ink then carve it to "uncover" the areas where you want the *first* color to show through.

Wherever the block is left uncarved, it will print black, completely covering the first, brown color. Because most block printing ink is opaque, a second, darker color applied over a first, lighter color will completely cover the first (as long as the first color has dried thoroughly before it's overprinted).

Here, the details of the face and eyes and texture of the background have been carved.

10 Roll out the second-color ink.

11 Apply it to the block with the brayer.

With the block completely inked, it's easy to see what will print and what won't.

12 Set up the paper for the second color the same way you did the first, poking the registration pins through the reinforced pin holes you already created so the paper is positioned exactly the same way it was the first time.

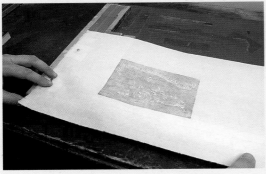

13 Set the ink block in the angle of the jig (making certain it's facing the same way it was for the first printing).

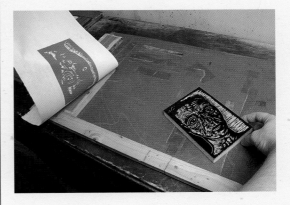

When everything's set properly, the two printings will register perfectly.

14 Slowly lay the paper over the block.

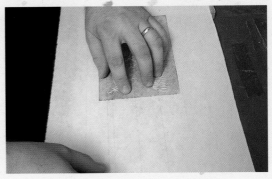

15 Transfer the ink with the rubbing tool.

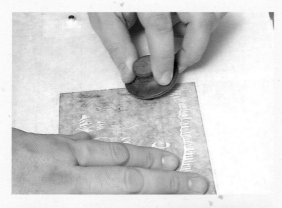

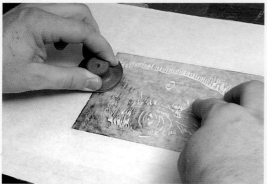

16 Work slowly and deliberately to avoid tearing the paper.

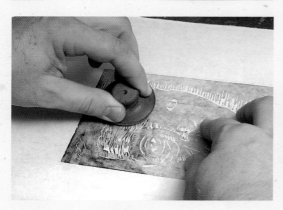

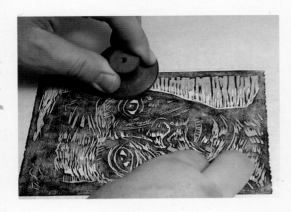

17 Carefully pull the print from the inked block.

The finished reduction print is rich and vibrant, even with only two colors.

In this two-color reduction print, a completely uncarved block was used to create a solid green background. The block was then carved and printed a second time with black ink.

Careful planning allows you to get create a variety of effects with the reduction print method. In this two-color reduction print, the rich highlights were achieved by printing green and black and cutting a minimal amount of white area. The white highlights were cut first then the green was printed; after it dried, the black was printed. This process created the impression that the white highlights were floating on top of the green and black.

5 Working with Wood

Wood is the traditional medium for block printing, and while the tools used for carving wood are different from those used to carve linoleum—and the carving techniques themselves differ somewhat—many of the printing materials and processes are the same. Using wood (the traditional Japanese technique is known as *moku hanga*) allows an artist to create prints with finer detail than is possible using linoleum.

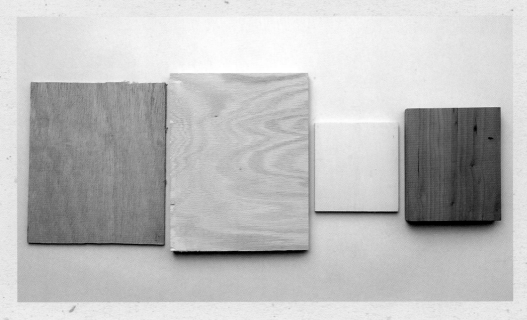

As with paper used for printing, there are a number of different types of woods suitable for creating printing blocks.

Luan is an inexpensive, easily carved wood that won't work well for detailed prints, but it's good for the beginner. The rough patches in the surface of luan can be filled with wood filler to create a better working surface. (Some artists prefer the grainy texture rough luan imparts to a print, but these areas can be difficult to carve.)

Standard wood putty can be used to smooth luan's rough areas and create a good carving surface, filling in the grain.

Preparing Luan

1 The first step in preparing luan is to use a plastic trowel (not metal, which can gouge the wood) to smear the putty onto the rough patches.

2 Use a wiping motion to work the putty smooth, covering the spots that need attention.

3 Apply as much putty as you need to.

4 Work the putty as smooth as possible, eliminating ridges and gaps.

5 When all the rough areas are covered, let the putty dry.

The putty will lighten considerably when it's dry, which should take at least an hour, depending on how thickly it was applied. Placing the wood in the warm sun will help it dry more quickly.

6 If there are still rough areas after the first coat of putty, apply patches to smooth them out and let the piece dry again.

7 Sand the dried putty with fine-grit sandpaper (it's best to sand the surface outdoors). Then wipe the wood with a rag or paper towel to remove the dust.

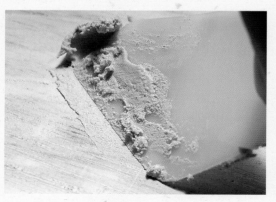

A puttied and sanded piece of luan makes a good material for carving and printing.

If you want to work with wood successfully, you should invest in a good set of wood-carving tools. Inferior tools will make for a frustrating experience, and you'll likely quit before you've had the chance to do work you're happy with.

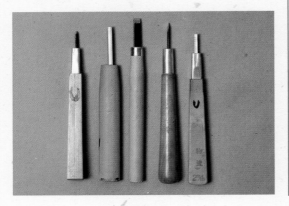

Unlike linocut tools, the cutting blades of wood-carving tools are usually made of steel and are meant to be sharpened when they become dull. Prepare to spend at minimum around $20 for a single good wood-carving tool, or $60 for a decent starter set. As with linocut tools, V-shaped and U-shaped gouges are most useful. A bull-nosed chisel and a knife are also in most woodcarvers' tool kits.

Other Wood Choices

Shina. A fine-grain plywood, easy to cut, dense, and relatively affordable, shina is an excellent, versatile wood for block printing. It's highly recommended for most purposes.

Birch Plywood. Finished birch plywood is another good choice for beginners. It's inexpensive and readily available—a 4-by-4 sheet can be cut up and goes a long way. The grain of birch plywood will be visible in prints, which can be a desirable effect.

Solid Cherry. This top-of-the-line wood is very hard and can be cut well only with high-quality tools. Consequently, it will hold extremely fine details and is a favorite of advanced wood block printers.

Maple. A premium wood, maple holds fine detail, and is also a favorite of expert printmakers.

Traditional two-part wood-carving tools are among the finest made. The edge of this tool is honed using a leather honing block.

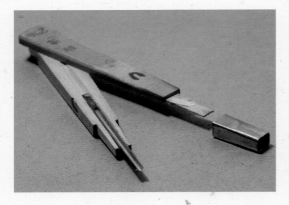

The handle of a standard wood-carving tool is meant to be cut down to perfectly fit the artist's hand.

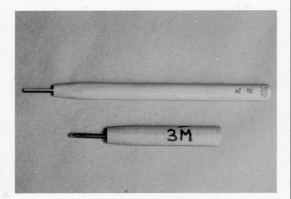

The uncut handle is too long to work with.

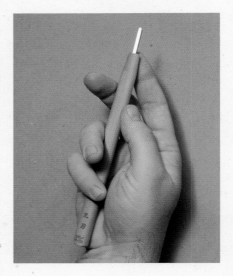

Cut the handle with a handsaw or table saw and sand the base so it fits along your forefinger and rests on the base of the thumb, as shown. A proper fit is important for both comfort and safety.

An important wood block carving aid is a bench hook. It's available from block print supply retailers. This tool is essential for wood carving; it will save time and make the carving process much safer.

With the hook's lip against the edge of your work surface and a corner of the block inserted between the hook's top pieces, you can carve by pushing away from you with the tool while the hook holds the block in place. Never carve a wood block while holding it in one hand and carving with the other—it's too easy for the tool to slip and cut you. Remember that wood-carving tools are extremely sharp and can cause serious injury.

Carving Technique

1 Hold the wood-cutting tool as you would a linocut tool, using both hands, guiding the tool with one finger placed on the top of the tool. Make small and deliberate cuts—there's a greater chance of slipping and carving what you don't want to carve if you work too fast. You may need to apply a bit more pressure to cut wood than you need to cut linoleum.

2 To cut away large areas of wood, first score the area with a knife.

3 Make shallow cuts in one direction.

4 Then make cuts in the other direction, creating crosshatching.

5 Then use a bull-nose chisel to lift away the tiny bits of wood you created—you are almost skimming the pieces from the block. Never wiggle the tool to make a cut; if you can't remove a bit, carve it into smaller pieces and try again.

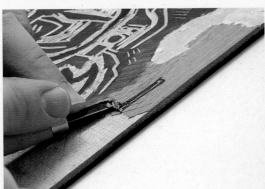

6 As with linoleum, you don't have to cut deeply. Carving deeply can damage the tool or the block itself.

7 As always, it's best to make small, precise cuts even when you're removing relatively large areas of wood.

8 You just need to eliminate the surface of the wood in order for the area to not print.

9 A small, sharp V-gouge will remove a very thin slice of wood. If it's sharp, it will cut the wood easily.

10 Use the tool to create fine detail. Remember to not carve too deeply.

11 You'll find that because the wood is harder than linoleum, you can make smaller, more delicate cuts, and your carving can be extremely fine.

12 As you work, you'll need to turn the block and fit different corners into the bench hook.

13 The biggest mistake beginning wood carvers make is trying to dig too deeply or work too quickly.

14 While you do need to apply steady pressure, the carving motions should be small and restrained.

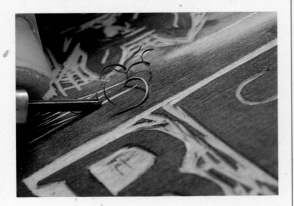

Water-based wood block inks in tubes are less viscous than other types of inks and can be helpful for indicating what you've already carved as you're working.

15 Pour a couple drops of ink on a paper towel or rag.

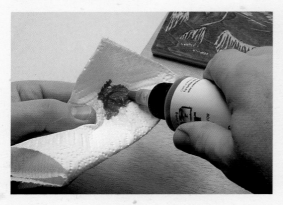

16 Wipe the surface of the block to color the areas that are left uncarved. Let the block dry before you resume carving—never cut wet wood.

17 This broad U-shaped tool will remove relatively thick slices.

18 It is useful for cutting away larger areas of the block while leaving thin strips that will add texture on the final print.

Small, precise cuts will help create a finely detailed image.

19 Use pieces of cardboard to raise a carved wood block up to the level of the side-pieces of the jig to make it easier to print. Tape the cardboard in place so it doesn't slip during printing.

20 An effective registration technique when using thin paper and printing small editions involves tacking the paper in place with pushpins and marking and reusing the holes.

21 Square the edges of a small stack of printing paper that's been torn down so all the pieces are the same size.

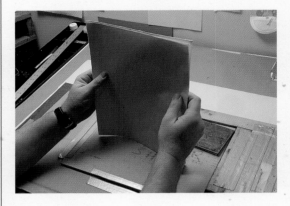

22 Put the uninked block in the jig and place the paper stack on top so that the top edge of the paper lies across the jig's top wood piece.

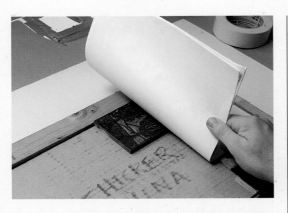

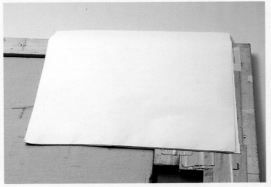

24 The top edge of the stack of paper should lie on top of the strip of tape.

23 Lift up a corner of the stack and apply a strip of masking tape to the raised piece.

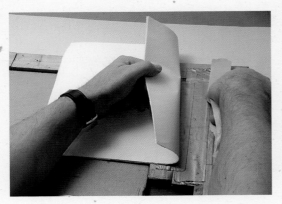

25 Tack the stack of paper in place, making sure you press the pins through the paper and the masking tape and into the wood.

26 Use two pushpins to hold the paper in place.

27 Now remove the pins and the stack.

28 Use a fine marker to circle the holes left in the jig by the pins. When you're ready to print, reuse the holes left in the paper and wood to keep everything registered.

29 Place one piece of paper over the block.

30 Tack the paper to the jig using the same holes you already made.

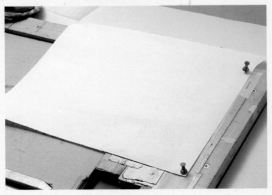

31 Then lift the paper and remove the block.

32 Ink the block as you would with linoleum then place it back in the angle of the jig, being careful not to mark the paper with the ink.

This registration works well for smaller blocks and editions.

33 Gently lay the paper over the block.

A baren is usually used to print wood blocks. This one, made of bamboo, helps to transfer the ink evenly to the paper.

34 Hold the baren as shown, with fingers curled around the handle and the thumb tucked in. This grip effectively transfers the weight of your hand and shoulder into the baren.

Don't grip the handle between the thumb and forefinger.

WRONG

Don't smash the baren down with the palm of your hand.

WRONG

35 When using a baren, it's best to place a piece of cellophane or ategami (a waterproof paper used for just this purpose) on top of the printing paper—especially if the printing paper is very thin. The cellophane will help distribute the weight of the rubbing evenly, keep the baren dry, and prevent paper tearing or roughening.

36 Transfer the ink by rubbing the baren over the surface of the block. The tool's shape will help you keep it even with the surface of the paper. Make smooth, circular motions, changing direction often.

37 Make sure you've transferred ink from across the entire block. When you've finished, remove the cellophane.

38 Slowly pull the print.

Kento Registration

The simple, traditional way of registering wood block prints known as *kento* involves leaving small portions in one corner and along one edge of the block uncarved.

The paper is then carefully positioned so that one of the corners is aligned with the block's corner mark …

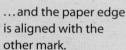

…and the paper edge is aligned with the other mark.

The paper (and cellophane) is held in place while the ink is transferred. If all the paper sheets are torn down to the same size, positioning them along the kento marks will help ensure that the printed area is positioned in the same place on every sheet.

Gallery of Annotated Prints

"Still Life with Cookies and Muffins" woodcut

Rich texturing brings this image to life and keeps the block interesting and expressive.

"Loosely After Durer" woodcut

An homage to Albrecht Durer and his "Rhinoceros" print using an animal native to North America. Durer added an extra horn to his rhino, and so this creature has one, too. A great example of the use of black and white and positive and negative areas, this piece was cut in shina using U and V gouges and a knife.

"Sun Woman" woodcut

A two-color reduction print—the color adds an interesting counterpoint to the black ink and white paper.

2/8   SUN WOMAN   Bob C

"Yautz's Farm" linocut

A dark and brooding print, influenced by the work of Fritz Eichenberg, with a mysterious, abstract quality given to a familiar scene.

"Late Dusting" linocut

A small park after a March snow. Strong lines and contrast give this piece a graphic look. The sketch in this case looked very much like the final print.

"Pear and Bottle" woodcut

Two simple objects with pop. Note how the subjects lean slightly
in opposite directions to avoid the sense that they are frozen.
This carving was made on prepared luan.

3/6   PEAR AND BOTTLE   Bob Craig

"Derelict Corral" linocut

Many barriers—fences, trees, power lines—are emphasized in this dense and textured print. Both ground and sky are given equal attention. Carved on goldcut linoleum.

(Untitled) woodcut

The cutting tool—in this case, a small U gauge—was used like a pencil on this print to create a white line cut.

"Cityscape" linocut

Purely a design piece, with strong lines and contrast. Carved on battleship gray linoleum.

"Pablo's Cactus" woodcut

A tight little still life with a variety of textures and objects. Still lifes can be thought of as many different objects coming together to create one.

2/6   PABLO'S CACTUS

"Last Legs" linocut

A good example of working the entire block—every element in this landscape is of equal importance and so is alive and in motion. The cutting textures keep it lush and vibrant.

"Erethizon dorsatum" woodcut

A simple piece and a unique subject.

"Corvus corax" woodcut

From a series on North American wildlife. A raven can be a challenge because of its overall dark appearance. Simple contrast and white lines make this image work.

¹/5   Corvus corax   Bob C

"Roseland Lutheran Church, North Dakota" linocut

An attempt to convey the emptiness and scale of the North Dakota landscape in a small print. The church itself is pushed to the far right side to emphasize loneliness and abandonment. The heavy, dark ground anchors the print against a stormy sky.

(Untitled) linocut

Done as a demonstration print for an art fair. The highlights were cut out and a green print was made. Then anything that wasn't to be black was cut away, and the black was printed over the green. Simple, expressive, and effective.

"Ursus arctus" woodcut

Another simple but challenging print. Strong composition and lines are key here, helping to convey the enormous size of the creature. Carved on birch.

"Pear" linocut

Water-based inks were used for this piece, showing how vibrant and luminous they can be. The color adds energy to a simple subject.

3/6   PEAR   Bob Craig

"Grasshopper" woodcut

A fun print, with color laid down first and the creature printed in black on top. Cut with a single U gouge.

"Procyon lotor" woodcut

A few expressive cuts go a long way toward making a print work. Capturing the face and tail was key to illustrating this animal's character.

"Blues Man" woodcut

The colored decorative paper used here immediately made creating contrast a challenge. White ink was printed first, followed by black, creating an interesting mix of paper, process, and color. Note the signature stamp in the lower right, carved in linoleum.

"Sleepy Lot" linocut

An interesting texture can make even a subject as plain as a parking lot come alive. This scene was rendered in a loose and charged style—the abstraction is obvious, yet the image is still understandable. It's important for artists to inject themselves into the execution and design of their work.

ACE studio tour poster, original woodcut print

An example of how block printing can transfer to a graphic advertisement. The original woodcut was supplied to a designer, who created the poster, adding type and a logo. Both U and V gouges were used to cut the print.

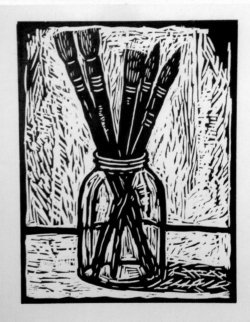

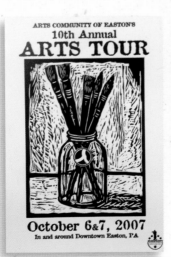

"Prairie Saplings" linocut

Three colors and a loose execution give this print a sense of
movement and life. Water-based inks were used.

"White Rhino" woodcut

This reduction print is all about texture. Highlights in the neck and a heavy, dark area on top keep the powerful face in the print frame. A small gouge was used throughout.

"Hercules Clouds" linocut

Created from a sketch that was done as a storm was approaching. Everything about these buildings and their surroundings seemed ominous, and the darkening sky added to the feeling. The cold, lifeless buildings contrast with the dark, moving sky.

Resources

McClain's Printmaking Supplies
imcclains.com

Blick Art Materials
dickblick.com

Speedball
speedballart.com

Daniel Smith Art Supplies
danielsmith.com

Utercht
utechtart.com

The Japanese Paper Place
japanesepaperplace.com

Renaissance Graphic Arts
printmaking-materials.com

Holbein Works
holbein-works.co.jp/english

Awagami Factory
awagami.com

Akua
waterbasedinks.com

Mclogan
mclogan.com